Things to Do

Things to Do

By Tina Lee

Pictures by Manning Lee

DOUBLEDAY & COMPANY, INC., GARDEN CITY, NEW YORK

TO RICKY AND BABBY

Contents

Things to Know About Things to Do

This book is planned to give you hours of fun and to show you how to change ordinary things into toys, gifts, and many attractive objects. Everything in the book is so easy you will be able to make them all by yourself. No special materials are needed, for almost everything is made from things found around the house, but you must begin right now to collect things you can use. Boxes of different kinds and sizes, tin cans, towel rolls, bottles, candy wrappers, bits of paper, stamps, fabric, ribbon and lace, braid, buttons, beads, and seeds are only a few things you will want. Magazines are full of "treasures," so clip everything from them that you can use, and don't forget to watch the mail for such things as oval-shaped envelope windows or areas of brightly colored paper so often found on advertising pieces. Start a treasure box in which to keep the things you've collected. Magazine clippings, papers, and pictures keep best between folded pieces of cardboard.

It is a good idea to start making the simple things first, such as paper playthings on page 17, and then make the more complicated ones. Read the directions carefully before you start and again, step by step, while you are working. Never try to work fast, and remember to allow time for glued things to dry.

Get to know your book by reading the Contents, which starts on page 6. It lists all the things to be found in the different sections of the book. The Index, which starts on page 62, is filled with ideas for using anything you might have. If you have some cans, look under the letter C until you come to the word "Cans." After the word you will see the numbers of the pages on which you will find things to make from them. Look under B for "Bags" and P for "Pictures" and so on. Use the Contents and Index often to get the most fun from your book.

If you are about to give a party, turn to page 42 for favors, decorations, and other ideas. For gifts to make, see the things starting on page 54. If you like to make doll clothes, six pages of exciting ideas and easy directions start on page 36. Many of these clothes are put together with one of the plastic adhesives. You will enjoy this kind of "sewing."

These are only a few things to know about THINGS TO DO, but as you look through it choose the things you like the best, assemble the materials you need for making them, and start having fun.

If you want to buy some things to work with, here are some suggestions:

Adhesives. You will enjoy working with SOBO, FIXSO, or EASY-SEW, which are the names of three inexpensive, easy-to-use adhesives found in department or five-and-ten-cent stores. They are excellent to use in making party hats and paper flowers, and fine for putting doll clothes together instead of sewing. They are colorless, never show on paper or cloth, and hold everything together firmly. EPOXY is the name of a wonder adhesive that sticks anything to anything, even tin to glass. Use it on the bird feeder, tin candlestick, or on anything that is hard to glue. Directions for use come with these products.

Rubber cement is a good all-round adhesive. It can be used on paper or cloth and is especially good for large surfaces such as when covering boxes. Any excess can be squeezed out around the edges and wiped away without leaving a mark.

Papers. Many useful papers can be bought from art-supply shops or department stores. One of the best is called Bristol board. It is white and stiff, and comes in several weights and surfaces in a wide price range. It is useful for making place cards, stand-up animals, paste-up pictures, furniture, and place mats.

Tracing paper is another useful one. It is something like tissue paper but more transparent and much stronger. It comes in tablets of various sizes. It makes fine butterflies, bird wings, pleated fans, flowers, and thin place mats.

Tissue paper can be bought in rolls of assorted colors as well as glitter-covered. These are fun to use for flowers and party hats. Rolls of heavy glazed paper in beautiful colors are lovely for many things, such as for lining boxes or making furniture like the desk on page 32.

Colors. Crayons, colored pencils, colored drawing inks, and water colors are all fun to use, but for real covering power show-card colors are the best as they are quite thick and they dry to an even mat finish. Varnish comes in almost any color, is easy to use, and usually dries overnight with fine results. Try it on tin or glass. Clear shellac, while not a color, is good to know about as it is useful in coating painted things such as trays and boxes. It dries quickly to a lovely gloss and acts as a protection.

TINA LEE
Boxwood Farm

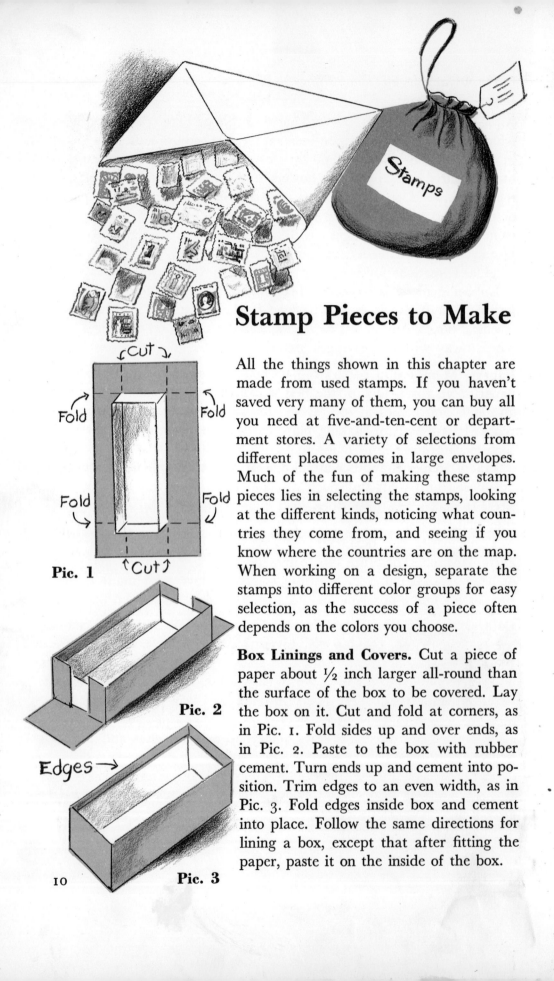

Stamp Pieces to Make

All the things shown in this chapter are made from used stamps. If you haven't saved very many of them, you can buy all you need at five-and-ten-cent or department stores. A variety of selections from different places comes in large envelopes. Much of the fun of making these stamp pieces lies in selecting the stamps, looking at the different kinds, noticing what countries they come from, and seeing if you know where the countries are on the map. When working on a design, separate the stamps into different color groups for easy selection, as the success of a piece often depends on the colors you choose.

Box Linings and Covers. Cut a piece of paper about ½ inch larger all-round than the surface of the box to be covered. Lay the box on it. Cut and fold at corners, as in Pic. 1. Fold sides up and over ends, as in Pic. 2. Paste to the box with rubber cement. Turn ends up and cement into position. Trim edges to an even width, as in Pic. 3. Fold edges inside box and cement into place. Follow the same directions for lining a box, except that after fitting the paper, paste it on the inside of the box.

Pic. 1

Pic. 2

Edges →

Pic. 3

10

Button Box. Face-powder boxes are fine to cover as they are well made and will last for quite awhile. Paint the bottom of the box with show-card color or enamel. Cover the lid with stamps of various colors, selecting carefully so that you can arrange them in a pleasant pattern. Start near the center and glue the stamps in position, overlapping wherever you like. When the box is covered cut the overhanging pieces even with the edge of the lid, as in Pic. 1. Cover with two coats of clear shellac.

Cut here

Pic. 1

Pillbox. Paint the inside of a tiny tin or paper box with a bright-color enamel, using a very small brush. Cover both top and bottom of the box with stamps, chosen with the size of the box in mind. Sometimes one very pretty stamp is large enough to cover the entire top or bottom. When the box is completely covered cut away any overhanging pieces around the edges as in Pic. 1. Cover with two coats of clear shellac.

Trinket Box. Line both top and bottom of a strong, oblong box, following directions on page 10. Cover the top with overlapping stamps and cut away any overhanging edges, as in Pic. 1. Coat twice with clear shellac. A box like this can be used for cigarettes, jewelry, ribbons, small papers, or almost anything you want to keep in a safe place. Nearly everyone could find a use for it.

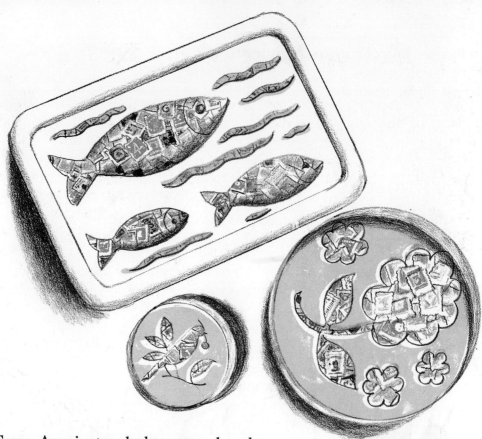

Trays. Any size tray looks pretty when decorated with overlapping stamps or with designs cut from stamps. Directions for making these designs are given on the facing page, and some patterns to trace are on pages 14 and 15. An easy way to decorate a tray, without using designs, is to cover it completely with overlapping stamps, paste a band of gold paper around the edge, and coat with clear shellac.

Pencil Holder. Remove the top from a can of frozen orange juice. Leave the inside as it is, or paint with bright-colored enamel. Cover the outside with overlapping stamps and trim edges, both top and bottom, even with the can. Finish top with a band of gold paper held in place with rubber cement. Coat twice with clear shellac.

How to Make Stamp Designs

Use a piece of typewriter paper or any other thin paper, slightly larger than your design is to be. Paste overlapping stamps on a portion of it large enough to cover the design you want to make, as in Pic. 1. Turn the paper stamp-side down and draw your design on the white side, as in Pic. 2. Now, cut out on the penciled lines, as in Pic. 3. Turn this cutout over and you will have a design made entirely of stamps. Add all details on the stamp side, such as eyes, wings, or whiskers in pencil, paint, or ink. Use these designs to decorate trays, boxes, letter holders, and such. The fish on the tray shown are made in three sizes, from yellow and orange stamps. The waves are cut from green ones. The flowers on the round tray can be made from different shades of pink and red; the leaves, green. Do some designs of your own or use the patterns to trace on the next pages.

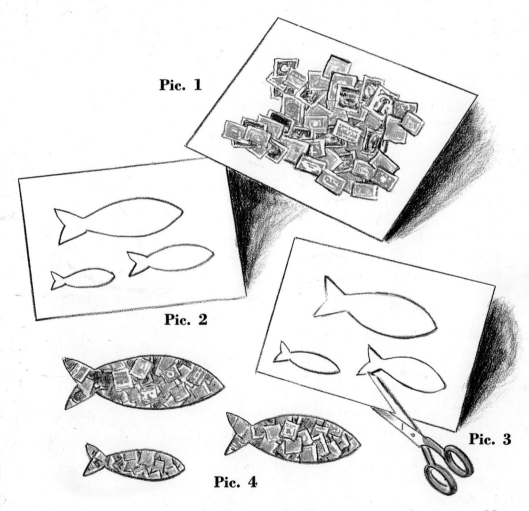

Pic. 1

Pic. 2

Pic. 3

Pic. 4

13

Patterns

Angel

Bud

Daisy

Star Flower

Fish

Rooster

Wren

14

Patterns

Angel

Bud

Daisy

Star Flower

Fish

Rooster

Wren

14

to Trace

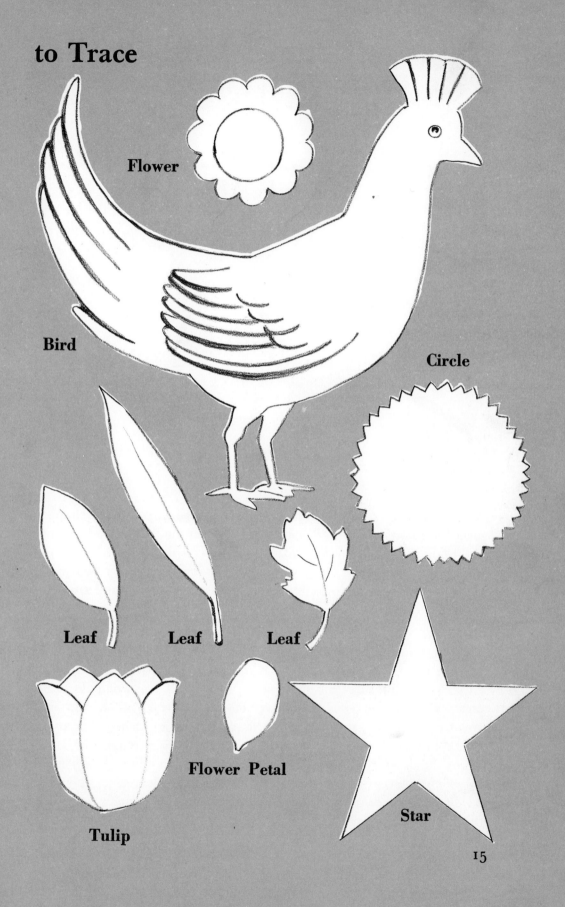

Flower

Bird

Circle

Leaf

Leaf

Leaf

Tulip

Flower Petal

Star

15

Paper Things to Make

Pic. 1

Making things from paper is easy, and it is always fun to change a piece of plain paper into something interesting by folding, cutting, and adding a bit of color. Make the things on these pages, then think up some of your own. Once you begin playing with paper you will be surprised by the different effects you can get by folding and cutting in a variety of ways.

Pinhole Lamp Shade. The way the light shines through this shade is what makes it really pretty. To make it, start with an inexpensive paper shade. Be sure that it is paper, as a cloth one won't do. Lay a piece of tracing or tissue paper over Pic. 1, and trace all the lines with a soft pencil. Now, transfer to the shade by putting pencil side against it and drawing over the pencil lines that show through the paper. Space the designs evenly before transferring. Use a pin or heavy needle to punch holes, as shown by dots in Pic. 1. The thickness of the pin or needle determines the size of the holes as well as how much light comes through the shade.

Peephole. It is fun to look through a peep-hole and pretend that it is a microscope. Make one by punching a hole in a heavy piece of paper. Use it for looking at any small object.

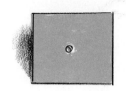

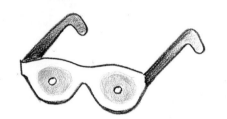

Pic. 1

Peephole Glasses. Draw around a pair of real glasses to get a good shape. Add side-pieces to look like Pic. 1. After you have cut the glasses out, fold the sidepieces back. Color the lenses and cut peepholes in them.

Pic. 2

Wire →

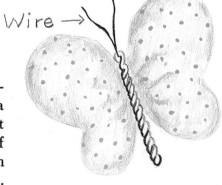

Butterfly. Fold a small square of glitter-covered tissue paper in half and draw a shape like Pic. 2. Cut it out and pleat slightly through the center. Bend a piece of pipe cleaner in half for a body, and run a fine wire through the bend, as in Pic. 3. Slip the wings through this body and twist both ends firmly to hold them in place.

Pic. 3

Pic. 5 ← Fold

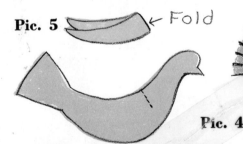

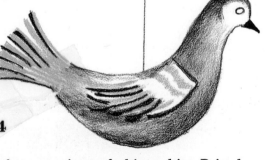

Pic. 4

Bird Mobile. This bird is made from a piece of thin, white Bristol board, but it can be made from almost any kind of plain or fancy paper. Draw and cut out a bird shape, *slit the back and clip the tail* as in Pic. 4. Cut wings from a piece of folded paper, as in Pic. 5. Curl tail and wing tips by running them between your thumb and a table knife. Open wings and insert into slit, holding in place with a touch of paste. Hang from a fine thread attached to the center back.

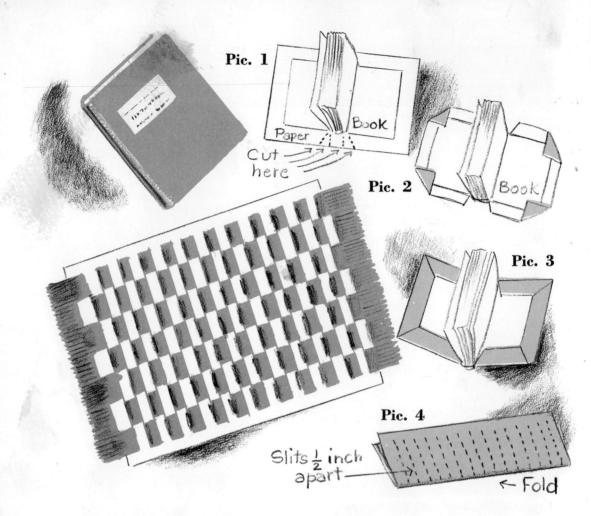

Pic. 1

Paper Book

Cut here

Pic. 2 Book

Pic. 3

Pic. 4

Slits ½ inch apart

← Fold

Book Cover. Any strong paper can be used to make a fine book cover. Open the book and lay it flat on the covering paper which has been cut about 1½ inches larger than the book on all sides. For a small book allow less than 1½ inches. Lay the book in the center of the paper. Cut out at the backbone, as in Pic. 1, and fold the little flaps flat against the paper. Fold outside corners, as in Pic. 2. Turn the remaining paper toward the inside of the book, as in Pic. 3. Fasten together at corners with a bit of rubber cement. Make a pretty label for the front of your book.

Place Mat. Start with a piece of white paper which measures 12 by 9 inches. Fold to measure 12 by 4½ inches. Rule a ½-inch border on the three open sides. Cut slits ½ inch apart, as in Pic. 4. Cut seven strips of colored paper to measure 1 by 14 inches. Weave these through the slits and fringe the ends so that the mat looks like the large picture. For a mat that is easier and quicker to make, cut the slits farther apart and the strips wider. Try making these mats from pieces of fabric for a different effect.

18

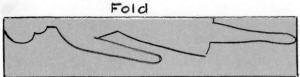

Fold

Pic. 1

Jiffy Paper People. To make paper people in a hurry, fold a piece of paper in half and draw a half figure, as in Pic. 1. Cut out, open up, and draw on details. You might find it amusing to use a thin layer of cotton for hair and bits of cloth for clothes.

Turtle. Fold a piece of heavy white paper in half and draw a shape, as in Pic. 2. Cut it out. Bend legs under, head up, and color to look like a turtle. For a stiffer turtle make a pattern on thin paper and transfer it to a piece of Bristol board.

Dog. Cut two papers, one 3 inches square, the other 1 by 2 inches. Fold in half and draw the dog's body on the larger one, the head on the smaller, as in Pic. 3. Cut out. Glue the head to the body as in the large picture and color to look real.

Leaves. Place any well-shaped leaf under a piece of tissue or tracing paper. Rub over the paper with colored pencil or crayon. All the veins will show through in a nice design. Draw around other leaves and color them as you like. Cut them out and use them as decorations.

Fold

Pic. 2

Fold

Fold

Pic. 3

Glue here

19

Pictures You

Mirror Pictures. Find a small, pretty picture, cut from a magazine or Christmas card, and paste onto a handbag mirror. Fasten a small curtain ring to the back with Scotch tape for a hanger. The attractive thing about these pictures is the way the mirror acts as a frame.

Crab-can Portrait. Both fresh crab meat and oysters come in cans with large cellophane windows on the top. The frame for this portrait is made from one of these. Open the can by removing the bottom, and draw around it to get a piece of pasteboard the same size. Cover the board with a pretty portrait or other picture. Fasten this to the bottom of the can with Scotch tape, as in Pic. 1, being sure the picture shows through the window. Paint the can any color that looks well with the picture. Scotch-tape a small curtain ring to the back for a hanger.

Sardine-can Picture. Fold a strip of velveteen around the sides of a clean sardine can, as in Pic. 2. Fasten it in place with rubber cement. Cut out or make a picture the size of the bottom and slip it inside the can, holding in place with a touch of cement. Tinsel used around this frame makes it a real Christmas picture.

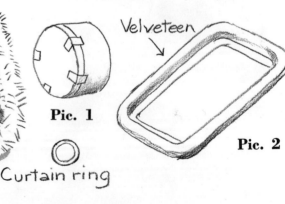

Pic. 1

Curtain ring

Velveteen

Pic. 2

20

Can Make

Can-top Picture. For a small picture use the top from a frozen-fruit-juice can. The one shown is of a gay clown, but you can fill the space with anything you like. Paint it with show-card colors. A little soap on the brush will make the paint stick.

Ham-can Picture. For a deep-set picture use the bottom of a ham can. Usually, you will need to paint it only on the outside. Now, either paint a picture on the inside or use one cut from a magazine or card. A Madonna, angel, or Santa Claus, backed by leaves and flowers, is nice for Christmas, or use a bunny watching a nest of brightly colored eggs for Easter.

Oval-can Picture. Cover the sides of a small oval can with a strip of foil, kept in place by a touch of cement. Paint a tiny flower picture inside or line the inside bottom with foil to use as a doll-house mirror.

Make-believe Ivory. Paint pictures with water colors on left over slivers of soap. It will be more fun than you expect, and when finished they look like little pieces of jade or ivory. With a heavy needle make a hole and add a loop of colored yarn for a hanger.

Pic. 1

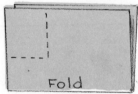

Fold

Pic. 2

Fold↗

Pic. 3

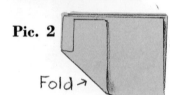

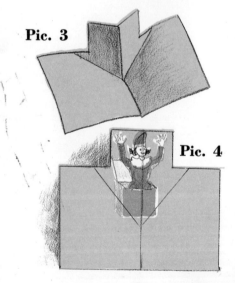

Pic. 4

Jump-up Pictures

These pictures can be very gay, for they should, whenever possible, contain a surprise such as a Jack-in-the-box, a Santa Claus, witch, cat, monkey, tulips, or other flowers. Use these pictures for place cards, Valentines, Christmas cards, or something that's fun to make and play with. Make them in any size, from the tiniest to a very large one for two children to open at a party. The Jack-in-the-box and tulips shown start with a piece of white paper 8½ by 11 inches. Fold to measure 8½ by 5½ inches. Cut as shown by dotted lines in Pic. 1. This leaves a high part, which, when the paper is opened, comes in the middle. Fold, as in Pic. 2. Now fold the high part toward the inside, as in Pic. 3, and crease well. Open and draw a figure, flowers, or bird on the high part, as in Pic. 4. If possible, cut around the part of your picture that is drawn on the high center part, so it will look like the figures at the top of this page.

Stand-up Pictures

There are many ways to make pictures stand up, and a few easy ones are shown on this page. Try them all and decide which way you like best, though you will probably find them all useful at different times.

Fold Over. Use a heavy piece of paper, folded in half, on which to mount or draw a picture. Colored paper is nice to use as you can leave a border all around the picture to act as a frame.

Easel. Attach a stiff piece of paper, cut as in Pic. 1, to the back of any picture. It will act as an easel and make the picture easy to stand.

Side Fold. Cut and fold a picture, or the board for mounting one, as in Pic. 2. Fold back on dotted lines far enough to make it stand.

Tube Backs. Make cutout pictures of people, trees, animals, furniture, and cars. Make them stand by gluing small paper or pasteboard cylinders to the backs, as in Pic. 3.

Pic. 1

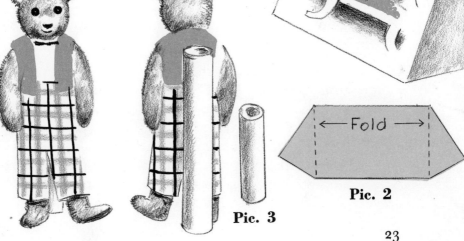

Pic. 3

Pic. 2

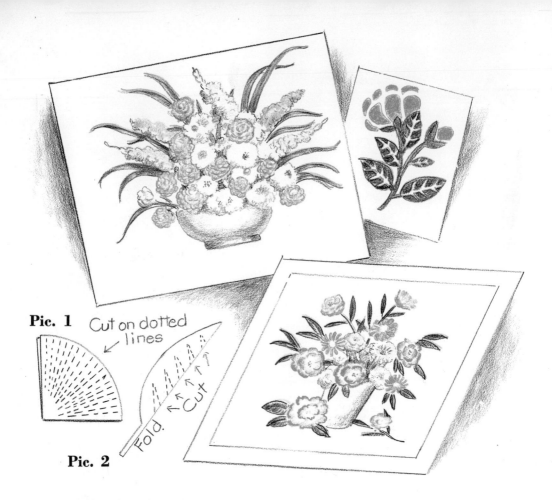

Pic. 1 Cut on dotted lines

Pic. 2 Fold. Cut

Paste-up Pictures. These are made from pieces of paper or parts of pictures cut from old books or magazines and arranged together to form a picture of your own. They are often called collage, which is a French word meaning pasting or gluing. The one at the top of the page is made of flowers cut from a seed catalogue. The leaves and vase are cut from colored paper. Arrange the pieces on white paper the way you want your picture to look and draw around them with a light pencil line. Paste the leaves in place first, then the vase, and finally the flowers. For a picture all your own, cut petal and leaf forms from colored paper and paste them into a picture.

Tissue-paper Picture. To make the flowers for this picture cut small colored-tissue-paper circles of three sizes. Fold each in half twice and cut as shown by dotted lines in Pic. 1. Open the circles and paste layers of one, two, or three to the paper where you want a flower, holding them together in the center by a touch of rubber cement. Fluff each flower by gently pinching the outside of the circles together. To make leaves, cut green-paper shapes, as shown in Pic. 2. Arrange flowers and leaves into a picture and paste into place.

24

Pic. 1

Scratch Pictures. Cover a piece of strong paper, such as Manila, with a thin layer of light-colored crayon, working it on in one direction. Now, cover a second time, working in the opposite direction. When this is done use a darker crayon to cover the light coating, pressing hard to get a heavy coat. With a heavy stub-pen point or manicure tool, used like a little shovel, scratch out the picture you want to make. You might find it amusing to draw the shape of an animal, fish, or bird in heavy black crayon, right on top of the other colors, and scratch out details such as eyes, scales, or feathers. Once you get the hang of doing scratch pictures you will enjoy making many of them.

Gauze Pictures. For a tiny picture which will look nice on your bureau, desk, or in a doll house, start with a stiff piece of gauze, such as you'll find on foot plasters of various kinds, as shown in Pic. 1. Draw a picture in very light pencil and work over it in colored thread, crayons, or both. The effect is lovely, much like a tiny needle-point embroidery. Make a mat and small frame for it.

25

Frames

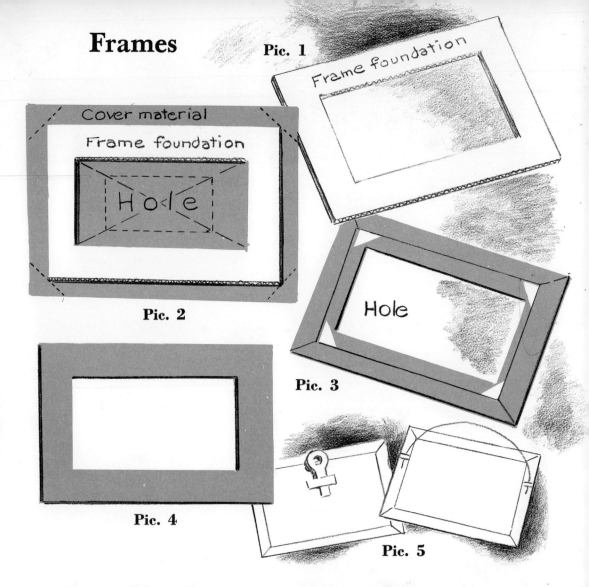

Pic. 1

Cover material

Frame foundation

Hole

Pic. 2

Frame foundation

Hole

Pic. 3

Pic. 4

Pic. 5

How to Make a Frame. It is useful to know how to make picture frames, and easy, too. One of the best ways is to cut a piece of corrugated board to the size you want your frame to be. Cut a hole in the center for your picture to show through. This is the frame foundation and should look like Pic. 1. Spread one side of this with rubber cement and lay it, cement-side down, on the paper or cloth with which you are covering the frame. This should be cut larger than the frame foundation. Cut the covering on dotted lines, as in Pic. 2, removing the section marked "hole." Fold the edges over the frame foundation and glue neatly into place on the back, as in Pic. 3. When finished it should look like Pic. 4. After you have put a picture into the frame, cover the back with a piece of clean paper, held in place with rubber cement. Add an easel, as shown on page 23, or one of the hangers shown on page 29, attached as in Pic. 5.

26

"Silver" Frame. Cover a corrugated-board frame, as shown on facing page, with plain, regular-weight aluminum foil (not quilted) and, using an ordinary lead pencil, draw designs all over the frame. It is a good idea to plan your designs carefully and space them out on the frame before you begin using your pencil because mistakes cannot be corrected very easily. When finished this frame looks very much like a real engraved-silver one. It is especially attractive for framing a picture of a friend or member of your family.

Box Frame. Cover a small box lid with foil or colored paper, running the covering into the inside edges of the lid. It makes a pretty shadow box frame for a snapshot, photograph, painting, or magazine picture. Glue the picture to the inside.

Milk-bottle-cap Frames. Use these caps of different designs for simple frames. Paste a picture or a snapshot to the center of the cap and add a hanger to the back. Open some out flat for a different effect.

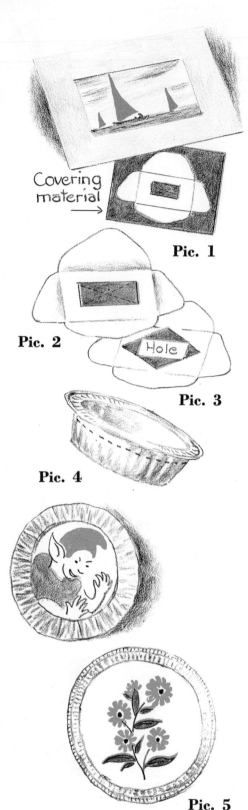

Covering material →

Pic. 1

Pic. 2

Hole

Pic. 3

Pic. 4

Pic. 5

Envelope Frame. Make one of these frames from almost any new envelope, large or small, heavy or light paper. What you choose to use will depend upon the picture you want to frame. They are all made the same way, and it is fun to experiment with different shapes and sizes. Open the envelope by unpasting the edges carefully. Cut a hole in the center big enough for your picture to show through. Cover the outside of the envelope with a coat of rubber cement, and lay it, cement-side down, on any cloth or paper you want to use for the frame covering, as in Pic. 1. Trim away any extra material from the outside edges of the envelope and cut material in hole on dotted lines, as in Pic. 2. Fold and paste material around hole into position, as in Pic. 3. Paste your picture to the inside of the frame so that it shows through the hole. Now paste the envelope flaps back into place. Add an easel or hanger.

Freezer-plate Frames. Many frozen foods come in plates and containers from which you can make picture frames. Watch for these and save the ones you want to use. Pie plates are particularly good for round frames, but oblong ones can be made from cheese-soufflé, macaroni, or scalloped-potato containers. The two shown on this page are made from frozen-chicken-pie plates. Cut off the top of the plate, as shown by dotted lines in Pic. 4. Paste a picture in the bottom and cover with a coat of colorless shellac. Add a hanger. Use the crimped rim which you cut off, for a round frame, as shown in Pic. 5. For bright-colored frames paint them with enamel. These rims make good rings for a toss game, too.

Box-lid Frames. These frames are quite easy to make. Use a shallow, medium-small-sized lid. Slit the corners, flatten the lid, then cut the corners on an angle, as shown in Pic. 1. Cover the lid with gold or some other colored paper, pasting over the edges, as in Pic. 2. Select a picture that will look well in this frame. Paste it in the inside bottom of the lid and fold the lid sides over it to form a frame. Glue it down firmly, as in Pic. 3. Add an easel or hanger.

If you want a tiny colorful inner frame, as shown in the picture at top of page, cut a piece of bright-colored paper the size of the bottom of the lid. Cut a hole large enough to show the picture, but about ¼ inch smaller all around than the hole left by the box frame when it is folded into place. Paste this around the picture before pasting the lid sides down, as in Pic. 4.

Pic. 1

Hangers.

1. Cut a shape from heavy Bristol board or cardboard and punch a hole, as in Pic. 5. Attach it to the picture with Scotch or masking tape.
2. Use a loop of heavy twine fastened to the picture by masking tape, as in Pic. 6.
3. Use a small curtain ring held in place with masking tape, as in Pic. 7.
4. Attach a length of wire or string from side to side on the back of the picture, as in Pic. 8.

Pic. 2

Pic. 3

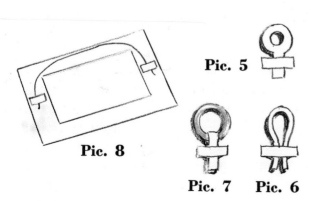

Pic. 8

Pic. 5

Pic. 7   **Pic. 6**

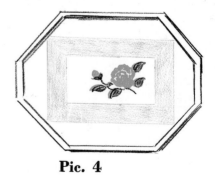

Pic. 4

Box Toys

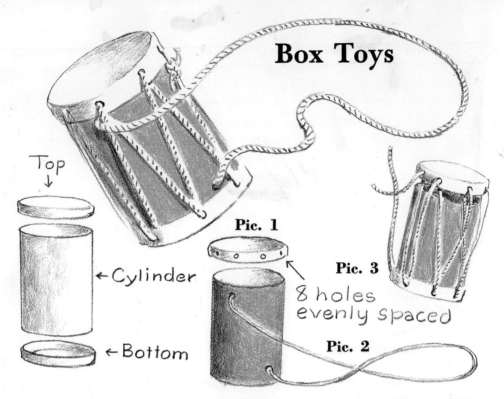

Top ↓

← Cylinder

← Bottom

Pic. 1

Pic. 3

8 holes evenly spaced

Pic. 2

Box Drum. Remove top and bottom section from an oatmeal cylinder-shaped box. Cut box to the height you want the drum. Cover with colored paper or paint with bright-colored enamel. Cover lid and bottom sides with a different colored paint or paper. Paste circles of white paper on ends to hide any printing. Punch eight evenly spaced holes in sides of top and bottom pieces as in Pic. 1. Make two holes in the cylinder and add a heavy cord, long enough to go around your neck, as in Pic. 2. Lace top and bottom to cylinder, as in Pic. 3, using a heavy string. Keep the lacing loose enough to make working easy until string has been put through all the holes. Now draw the string tight enough to hold top and bottom firmly to cylinder and knot securely.

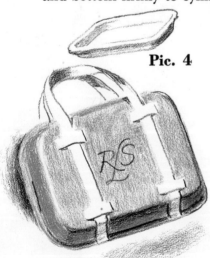

Pic. 4

Handbag. Hold two heavy paper fruit boxes, that look like Pic. 4, together and make straps and handles from contrasting colored Mystic tape, as in the large sketch. Make the handle section of double tape. Hold straps in place with small pieces of the tape. Add your initials for an extra touch. Bags like this, for carrying things, can also be made from two paper plates, two box covers of the same size, or frozen-food containers.

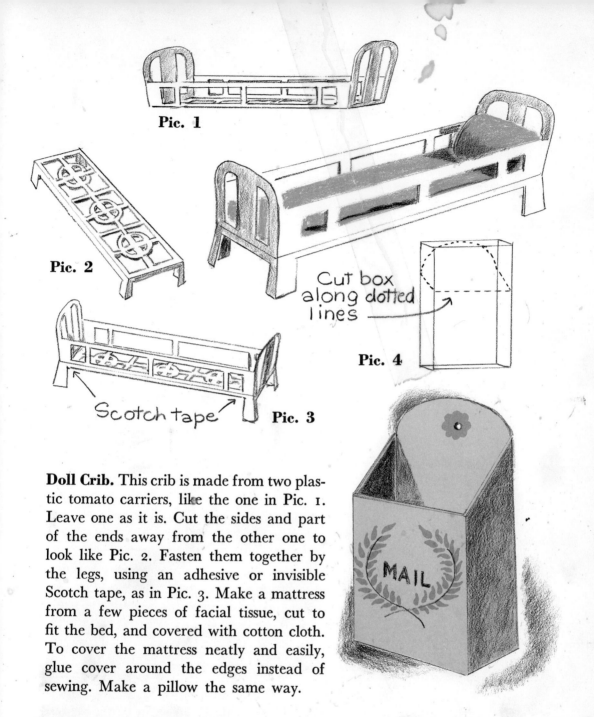

Pic. 1

Pic. 2

Cut box along dotted lines

Pic. 4

Scotch tape Pic. 3

MAIL

Doll Crib. This crib is made from two plastic tomato carriers, like the one in Pic. 1. Leave one as it is. Cut the sides and part of the ends away from the other one to look like Pic. 2. Fasten them together by the legs, using an adhesive or invisible Scotch tape, as in Pic. 3. Make a mattress from a few pieces of facial tissue, cut to fit the bed, and covered with cotton cloth. To cover the mattress neatly and easily, glue cover around the edges instead of sewing. Make a pillow the same way.

Mailbox. Cut a small, strong, cereal box as shown by dotted lines in Pic. 4. Round the back to look like the large picture. Cover with bright-colored paper, glued neatly into place, or paint with colored enamel. Orange with green leaves, white letters, and berries make a pretty combination. Punch a hole for hanging and decorate with a wreath. Add the word MAIL, or some initials. This is handy for mail, papers on your desk, or schoolwork. It makes a good gift, too.

Doll Swing. Any small, cube-shaped box can be converted into this swing. Round the front and back, cut sides down, and make leg holes, as in Pic. 1. Cover back, seat section, and front with gaily colored paper, such as red on a white box. Punch four holes in sides, as in Pic. 2. Turn front down to form a tray. Run heavy string through the holes and add a small brass curtain ring for hanging. Any small doll will enjoy this swing. For a larger doll use a heavy pasteboard box, cutting it in the same way as this small one.

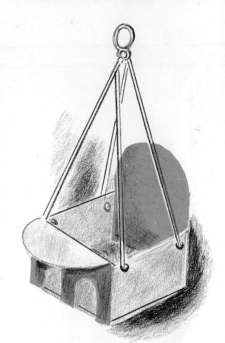

Cut along dotted lines →

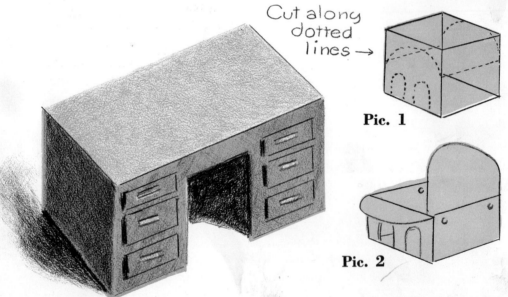

Pic. 1

Pic. 2

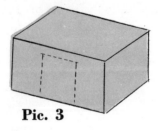

Pic. 3

Desk. The small desk on this page is made from a box which measures 3½ by 5½ by 2¼ inches, but it can be made in the same way from a larger box if you prefer. Cut a kneehole in the box, as in Pic. 3. Paint it or cover with glossy paper. Paint on drawers and add small pieces of gold paper or foil for drawer pulls.

32

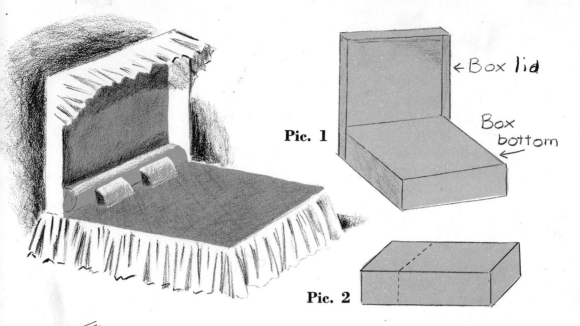

Pic. 1

←Box lid

Box bottom

Pic. 2

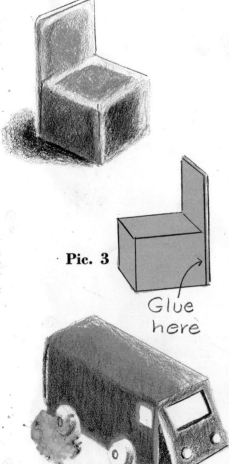

Pic. 3

Glue here

Box Bed. Make this bed from almost any small box with a shallow lid. The one shown here is of a size which goes well with the desk and chair on this page and the barrel chair on page 60. If your box is not a pretty color, you can cover the bottom and inside of the lid with gold or some other paper. Glue top and bottom together, as in Pic. 1. Cut the fluted part from two paper baking cups and paste these onto the bed for a flounce and canopy. The bolster is gold foil, rolled into shape over a pencil. The pillows are folded pieces of foil.

Chair. Cut 1½ inches from the end of a nail-polish box, as in Pic. 2. Cover with velveteen or other material. Cut a side section from the box and cover on both sides with the same fabric. This forms the chair back. Glue to seat, as in Pic. 3.

Truck. Paint a nail-polish box to look like any truck or car you want. The plastic wheels can be found in the tops of sauce bottles, such as soy. There's a hole in the center of these stoppers, so all you need for attaching is a small nail.

33

Telephone Booth. Glue the top of a quart or half-gallon milk carton together to look the way it did before it was opened, and hold in place with a clip until it is thoroughly dry. Cut as shown by dotted lines in Pic. 1. Paint the outside with colored enamel. Because these containers are very slick it may take two or three coats. Add the word TELEPHONE on all four sides, and add a thumbtack for a door pull. The door should open, as in Pic. 2.

Box Bus. Cut windows at both ends of an inverted shoebox and glue two pieces of cellophane in place for glass. Draw doors and windows on the sides to look like a bus. The six wheels can be made from reels on which home-movie film comes wound or from large pasteboard circles. Attach them by running two lengths of dowel stick, 1/8 inch thick, through the center of each wheel and through the bus from side to side. A small piece of Scotch tape wrapped on the dowel stick, near the wheel on the inside, will keep each one in place. Add a string for pulling.

Pic. 1

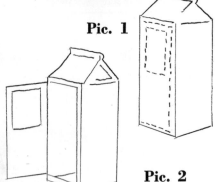

Pic. 2

34

Pic. 1

Carton Bird Feeder. Use a pointed can opener, like the one in Pic. 1, to punch four holes near the bottom of a cottage-cheese, yogurt, or sour-cream carton, and make two small holes near the top, as in Pic. 2. Attach carton with one of the all-purpose cements to the center of a tin lid or to an aluminum-foil or heavy paper plate. Paint the whole thing with two coats of enamel. Fill the carton part with birdseed. Cover, and hang by a wire run through the two small holes.

Tin-can Feeder. Make two holes in a large fruit-juice can and cut the top and bottom partway around. Then bend these back to look like Pic. 3. Enamel it a bright color. Run a strong cord through the holes and tie together inside the can. Tie a piece of suet to the cord, as in Pic. 4. Hang the feeder by the cord. Put birdseed inside the can every few days.

Pic. 2

Pic. 3

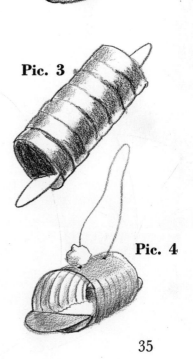

Pic. 4

35

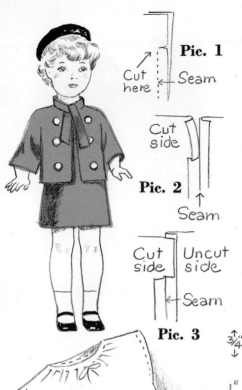

Pic. 1

Cut here — Seam

Cut side

Pic. 2

Seam

Cut side | Uncut side

Seam

Pic. 3

Easy-to-Make

These clothes are designed to fit a fifteen-inch doll. For a larger or smaller one, change the measurements according to her size. Many parts are put together with one of the new adhesives mentioned on page 9. It is fun and easy to use and makes a neat finish. To make a placket, sew the seam together and cut a small slit, as in Pic. 1. Press seam open, as in Pic. 2. Now lay cut side over uncut side, as in Pic. 3. When turned to the right side this placket looks like part of the seam.

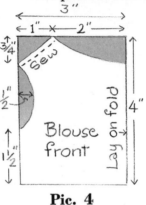

3″
1″ — 2″
3/4
Sew
1/2
Blouse front
Lay on fold
1 1/2
4″

Pic. 4

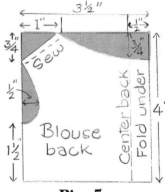

3 1/2″
1″ — 1/2″
3/4
Sew
3/4
1/2
Blouse back
Center back   Fold under
1 1/2
4″

Pic. 5

Blouse. Make pattern by marking two pieces of paper, as shown in Pic. 4 and Pic. 5. Pin each to a double thickness of fabric, laying center front on fold and cutting carefully. Sew underarms and shoulders together, hem armhole, and gather slightly around neck with large stitches of colored yarn. Turn ½ inch to the inside of left center back, extend right side under it for closing. Add a snap.

Pic. 6

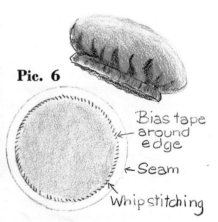

Bias tape around edge

← Seam

Whipstitching

Beret. Cut a circle of velveteen to measure 7½ inches across. Sew a piece of bias binding to the outside edge and whipstitch to the wrong side, as in Pic. 6. Run a 10-inch length of ¼-inch elastic through the casing and sew the ends firmly together. Add a feather if you have a tiny one.

Doll Clothes

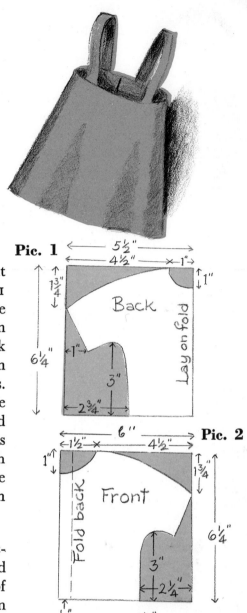

Jacket. Make the paper pattern for front and back by following directions on Pic. 1 and Pic. 2. Cut out and pin to a double piece of material, laying the center back on a fold. Cut fabric out carefully. Cut neck scarf to measure 15 by 1½ inches, fold in half to measure 15 by ¾ inches and press. Sew back to front at shoulder and side seams. Turn up 1-inch hem at bottom and ½ inch on sleeves. Turn fronts 1½ inches to the inside. Hold all these in place with an adhesive. Gather neck slightly across the back, slip between folded scarf, and fasten into place. Add six small buttons.

Skirt. Make pattern by following directions in Pic. 3. This is for both back and front. Cut front from a double thickness of cloth, laying center on fold. Cut the back in two pieces. Sew center back of skirt together, using ½-inch seam and leaving a 1¾-inch placket at the top. Sew side seams together and press open. Press one side of the placket even with the seam, extend the other side under it. Make a ¾-inch hem at the bottom and a ½-inch hem in the top. Add a snap at the top of the placket. Make two double straps ½ inch wide and 5 inches long. Fasten to skirt top.

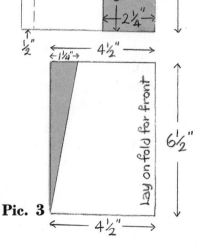

37

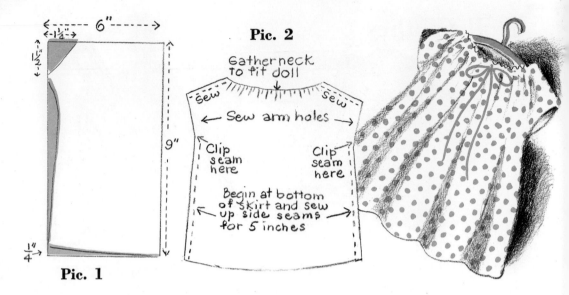

Pic. 2

Gather neck to fit doll

Sew

Sew ← Sew arm holes →

Clip seam here

Clip seam here

Begin at bottom of skirt and sew up side seams for 5 inches

6"

1¼"

1½"

9"

¼"

Pic. 1

Drawstring Dress. Make a pattern from a paper measuring 5 by 9 inches, marking as in Pic. 1. Cut out and pin to a double thickness of material, placing center on fold and cutting carefully. Make two of these. Sew them together, as in Pic. 2. Make a 1-inch hem at the bottom and a ½-inch hem at the top. Turn in seam width at armholes. Hold all these in place with an adhesive. Gather around the top with large stitches of wool. Tie in front.

Cape. Make paper patterns for back, front, and collar by following directions in Pic. 3 and Pic. 4, on this page, and Pic. 1, on the facing page. Pin front and back pattern to double thickness of material, laying center back on a fold. Lay back of collar on double thickness of contrasting material. Cut out. Sew side seams of cape together and press open. Turn 1-inch hem at bottom and fold in 2 inches at fronts. Turn a tiny hem toward the outside at the neck. Hold all these in place with an adhesive. Press well and fasten the collar into place on cape neck. A snap or tie at the neck will hold the cape on.

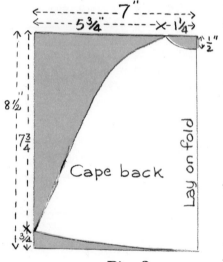

7"

5¾"

1¼"

½"

8½"

7¾"

Cape back

Lay on fold

¾"

Pic. 3

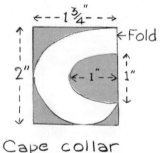

1¾"

2"

1"

1"

Fold

Cape collar

Pic. 4

38

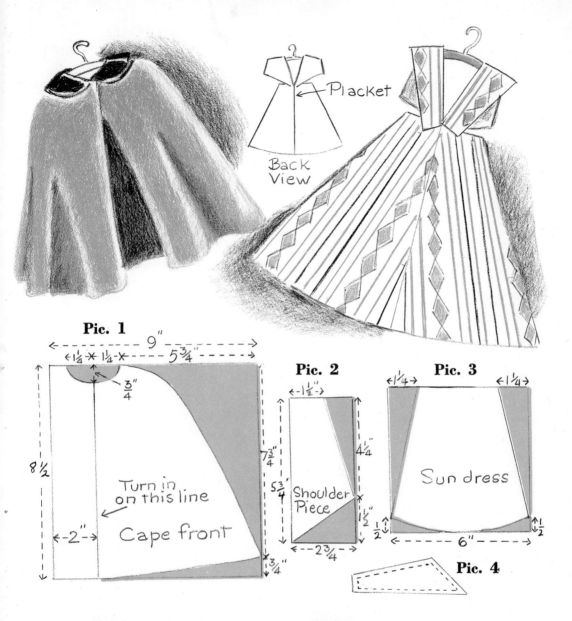

Pic. 1

Turn in on this line

Cape front

Pic. 2

Shoulder Piece

Pic. 3

Sun dress

Pic. 4

Sleeveless Sun Dress. Make paper patterns for skirt gores and shoulder pieces by marking two pieces of paper, as shown in Pic. 2 and Pic. 3. When cut out, pin to a double thickness of fabric, cutting around the shapes carefully. Do this twice, so that you have four of each piece. Sew the skirt gores together, leaving 1¾ inches open at the top of the back seam for a placket. Press all seams open. Make the placket by following directions on page 36. Make an inch hem at the bottom of the skirt and a ½-inch hem at the top, holding in place with adhesive. Sew shoulder pieces together, as in Pic. 4, leaving a place open for turning. Turn to the right side and press. Attach to top of skirt at front and back as in large sketch.

Clothes for a Teen-Age Doll

These clothes are designed for a 12-inch, teen-age doll. Many more clothes than those shown can be made from these patterns. The coats and dresses can be made long or short and a robe can be made from the coat pattern.

Coat. Cut paper patterns for both front and back of coat, as shown in Pic. 2 on facing page. Pin pattern to a double thickness of cloth, placing center back on a fold and cutting fronts in two pieces. Sew shoulder and underarm seams together, turn up ½-inch hem at bottom. Fasten contrasting bias binding up front, around neck and sleeves, holding in place with an adhesive. Add six buttons.

Pic. 1

Jacket back and front

Lay on fold for back
Cut open for front

Jacket. Make back and front of pattern, as shown in Pic. 1. Pin to a double thickness of fabric, placing center back on fold and cutting fronts in two pieces. Cut out carefully. Sew shoulder and side seams together. Bind all around with a piece of bias tape or a piece of bias-cut contrasting fabric. Hold in place with adhesive.

40

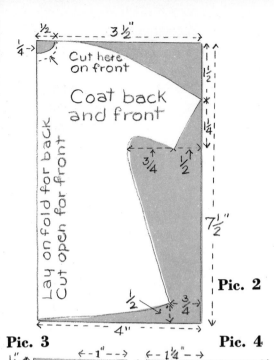

Pic. 2

Dress. Cut pattern for back and front, as shown in Pic. 6 and Pic. 7. Pin to double thickness of fabric, placing center front on fold and cutting back in two pieces. Sew center back together, leaving a 4-inch placket at the top. Turn one side of the placket even with the seam and extend the other side under it to form closing. Sew together at shoulders and underarms. Make a ¾-inch hem at bottom, a ½-inch hem on sleeves, and a tiny turn around the neck. Sew three snaps on back closing and add a string belt.

Pic. 3 **Pic. 4**

Pic. 5

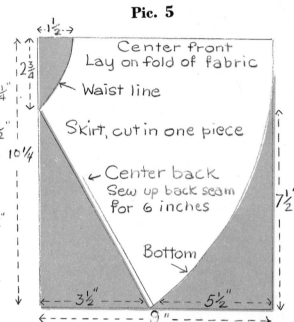

Pic. 6 **Pic. 7**

Evening Dress. Cut patterns for bodice and skirt as shown in Pic. 3, Pic. 4 and Pic. 5. Pin to double thickness of fabric, placing bodice and skirt front on fold. Cut back of bodice in two pieces. Make darts in bodice. Sew shoulders and sides together. Make tiny hems at neck and armholes. Seam skirt together, leaving a 1¾-inch placket. Seam skirt to bodice at waist. Make placket, as shown on page 36. Close dress with three snaps. Add trimming, such as lace or beads, or draw it on with sharp crayons.

41

Party Favors

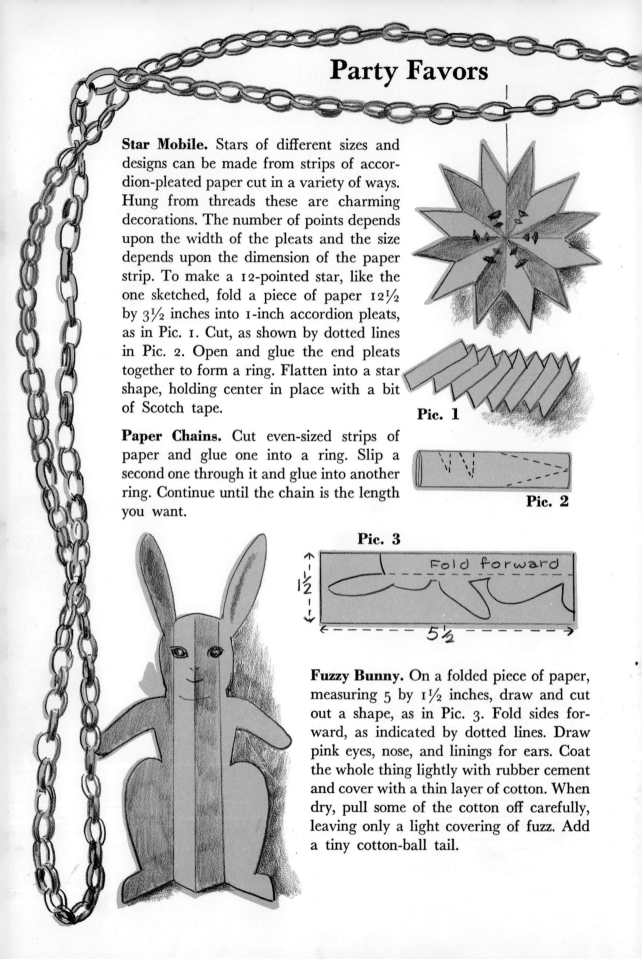

Star Mobile. Stars of different sizes and designs can be made from strips of accordion-pleated paper cut in a variety of ways. Hung from threads these are charming decorations. The number of points depends upon the width of the pleats and the size depends upon the dimension of the paper strip. To make a 12-pointed star, like the one sketched, fold a piece of paper 12½ by 3½ inches into 1-inch accordion pleats, as in Pic. 1. Cut, as shown by dotted lines in Pic. 2. Open and glue the end pleats together to form a ring. Flatten into a star shape, holding center in place with a bit of Scotch tape.

Paper Chains. Cut even-sized strips of paper and glue one into a ring. Slip a second one through it and glue into another ring. Continue until the chain is the length you want.

Pic. 1

Pic. 2

Pic. 3

1½

5½

Fold forward

Fuzzy Bunny. On a folded piece of paper, measuring 5 by 1½ inches, draw and cut out a shape, as in Pic. 3. Fold sides forward, as indicated by dotted lines. Draw pink eyes, nose, and linings for ears. Coat the whole thing lightly with rubber cement and cover with a thin layer of cotton. When dry, pull some of the cotton off carefully, leaving only a light covering of fuzz. Add a tiny cotton-ball tail.

and Decorations

Bird Cage. Put a piece of glitter-covered tissue paper in the bottom of a shallow box lid which is about ¾ inches deep and measures about 5¾ by 3¾ inches. Glue white-paper drinking straws to the inside of the lid, as in Pic. 1. Tie four straws, about 2½ inches above the lid, to the upright ones, knotting, as in Pic. 2. Add four more, in the same way, 2½ inches higher. Trim straws at the corners, leaving about ½ inch on each. Draw a small paper bird and glue it firmly to a straw. Slip it into the cage and tie securely at the sides. Finish the cage at the top by bending all the straws, carefully, toward the center, cutting them to an even length. Run a needle and thread through each straw, draw together, and tie. Add a curtain ring for hanging.

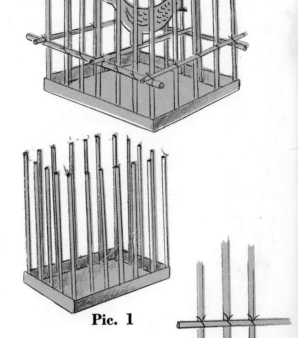

Pic. 1

Pic. 2

Pic. 3

Pic. 4

Pill-bottle Place Cards. Add amusing tops to little pill bottles and fill with tiny colored candy: Place them on cards lettered with guests' names. To make a poodle, draw a face on a strip of paper long enough to fit around the bottle when glued into a ring, as in Pic. 3. Add long, cotton-coated ears, paste into a ring, and slip onto the bottle top. Add a puff of cotton to the head and a tiny colored string bow.

Draw a chicken on a double piece of paper, as in Pic. 4. Color and paste the pieces together along head, front, and tail; slip over bottle top.

43

Cork Cat. Draw a cat face on the small end of a cork. Paste on green-paper eyes and black-paper ears. Add four toothpick pieces for legs and one for a tail.

Cork Elf. Add paper pieces for eyes, mouth, and ears. Attach a white cotton wig. Slip two whole and two half toothpicks into the cork for arms and legs. The cap is a double piece of velveteen, cut as in Pic. 1, and rubber-cemented together on the curved edge.

Cornucopia. Cut a half circle about 8 inches across. Attach a string hanger, as in Pic. 2. Roll into a cornucopia, overlapping about 4 inches, as in Pic. 3. Cement together and fill with candy, nuts, or tiny toys.

Baking-cup Basket. Run a pipe cleaner through the sides of a fluted-paper baking cup to form a handle. Add a paper flower.

Foil Basket. Cut the crimped rim from a frozen-chicken-pie plate. Then cut the rim in half and bend to form two handles. Fold the plate into a basket shape and cement the handles in place. Fill with real or fake flowers. Tie handles together with ribbon.

Tricorn Candy Holder. Cut the rim from a frozen-chicken-pie plate. Bend the plate to look like a tricorn, as in the large sketch on facing page. Paint black, and add a red-white-and-blue pleated-paper cockade. Fill with bright candies. Use for a Washington's Birthday party.

44

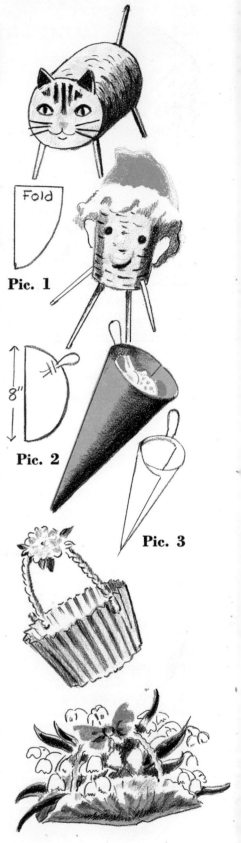

Pic. 1

Pic. 2

Pic. 3

Open end

Fold

Pic. 1

Paper Lantern. Fold a piece of white or colored paper in half and cut from folded side, as in Pic. 1. Open up and paste both end strips together to form a lantern shape. For a more melonlike shape, bend strips outward, running between thumb and first finger. Strings of these make-believe lanterns look very gay.

Flags and Pennants. Cut pennants from tissue paper of different colors and attach them to sticks, such as thin plant markers. Make them any size you need. Slogans and names can be drawn on them with crayons. The little flags are cut from a sheet of 80 flags which can be bought at five-and-ten-cent stores. Fasten each flag to a toothpick with a touch of cement. Use them to decorate cakes or stick one in a gumdrop and add to a place card.

Soap Boats. The boats are small cakes of floating, white soap, the sails are white shelf paper, held on by toothpicks. The square ones measure 2½ inches. Triangular ones are 5 by 5 by 2½ inches. The smaller one is 2½ by 3 by 1¾ inches. Put the boats in water and blow on the sails to make them travel. It is fun to race them at a party.

45

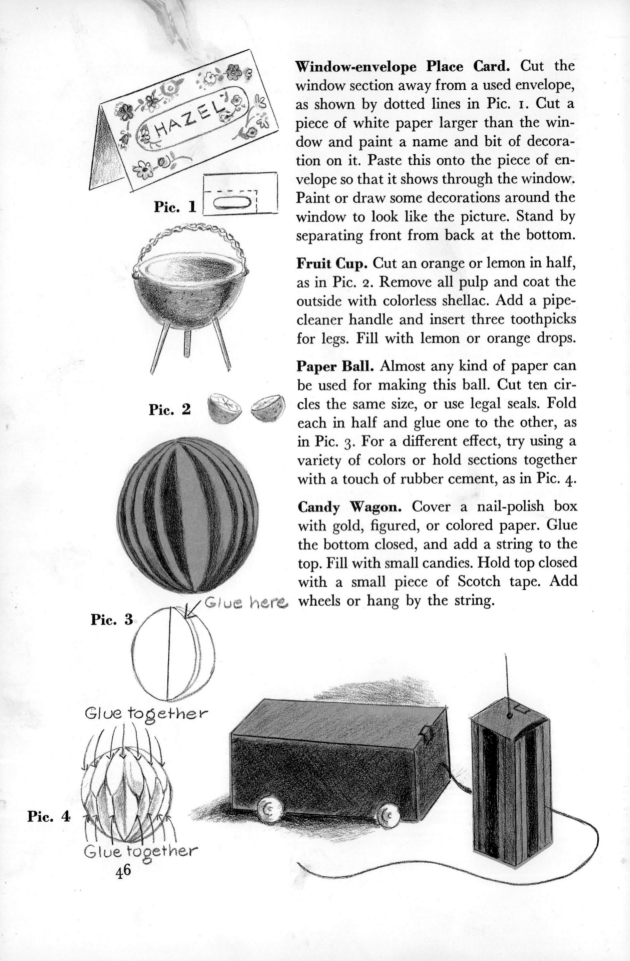

Window-envelope Place Card. Cut the window section away from a used envelope, as shown by dotted lines in Pic. 1. Cut a piece of white paper larger than the window and paint a name and bit of decoration on it. Paste this onto the piece of envelope so that it shows through the window. Paint or draw some decorations around the window to look like the picture. Stand by separating front from back at the bottom.

Fruit Cup. Cut an orange or lemon in half, as in Pic. 2. Remove all pulp and coat the outside with colorless shellac. Add a pipe-cleaner handle and insert three toothpicks for legs. Fill with lemon or orange drops.

Paper Ball. Almost any kind of paper can be used for making this ball. Cut ten circles the same size, or use legal seals. Fold each in half and glue one to the other, as in Pic. 3. For a different effect, try using a variety of colors or hold sections together with a touch of rubber cement, as in Pic. 4.

Candy Wagon. Cover a nail-polish box with gold, figured, or colored paper. Glue the bottom closed, and add a string to the top. Fill with small candies. Hold top closed with a small piece of Scotch tape. Add wheels or hang by the string.

Pic. 1

Pic. 2

Pic. 3

Glue here

Glue together

Pic. 4

Glue together

46

Stand-up Cat. Fold a 3-by-4-inch piece of Bristol board or other heavy paper, to measure 3 by 2 inches. Draw a cat body, as in Pic. 1, and cut out, making small slit in back, as shown. Color to look like a cat. Cut a tail and a head with a long tab, as in Pic. 2. Color these to go with the body. Insert tail in slit and glue in place. Glue the head tab to the back of the body, so cat looks like the picture. A black one makes a fine Halloween decoration.

Drinking-straw Triangles. Cut colored cellophane straws into 12, 2½-inch lengths. String three of them together to form a triangle. Make four of these. String them together to look like the lantern shape at the right.

Ice-cream-cone Carrier. In a shallow box lid, which measures about 5½ by 10 inches, cut five or six evenly spaced round holes, 1½ inches across, as in Pic. 3. Punch two holes in each corner and add two pieces of ribbon, long enough to go around your neck, as in Pic. 4. Decorate with streamers of different colors. Insert the filled cones into the holes. Makes serving easy.

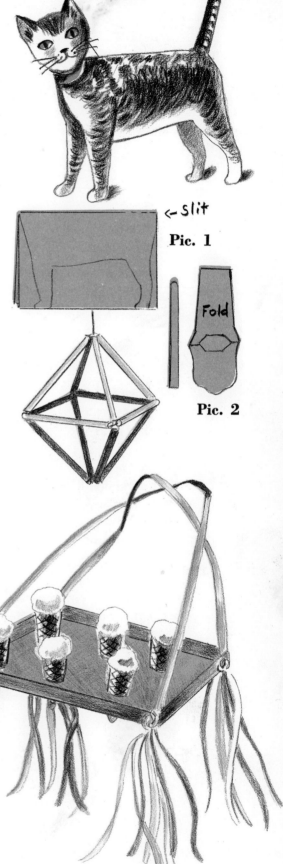

←slit

Pic. 1

Fold

Pic. 2

Pic. 3

Pic. 4

Candlestick. Cover a tin can with aluminum foil, turned carefully into the top and under the bottom. Fasten to a base made from an inverted frozen-chicken-pie plate. Cut a crimped edge from another plate. Cut center of plate, as shown by dotted lines in Pic. 1. Bend points up to hold candle, as in Pic. 2. Fasten to the top of the can with adhesive and use tinsel around the base and top.

Drum Candle. Paint a small tin can to look like a drum. Attach a piece of heavy string to the exact center of the inside bottom, with masking tape. Fill can with melted paraffin, warm enough to pour but not hot. Hold the string upright by attaching it to some object above the can until the wax is set. Cut string to wick length.

Pic. 1

Pic. 2

Hand Masks. Make these masks to wear on your hands for characters in your next puppet show. Use bags large enough to fit over your hand. Draw and paint the characters, using pieces of paper, cloth, beads, and feathers to make them more amusing. Ears can be cut separately and attached over the top edge, like the cat, or they can be flat pieces pasted to the front of the bag. The cat's tongue can be made of red paper, curled to stand away from the bag. "Miss Bear's" necklace is set with sequins. Larger masks, to be worn over your head, can be made from grocer's bags in the same basic way. Draw backs as well as fronts on these, and cut peepholes on a level with your own eyes.

48

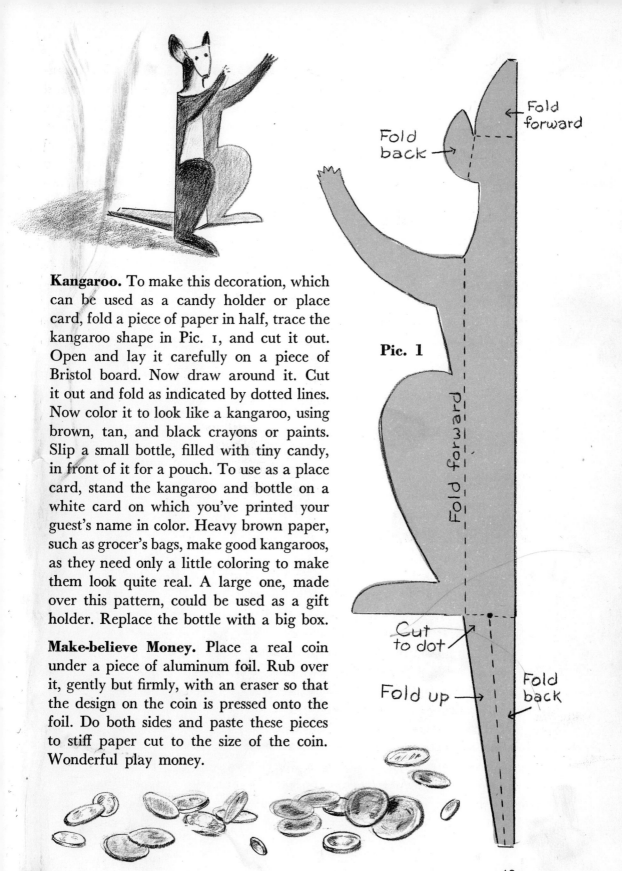

Kangaroo. To make this decoration, which can be used as a candy holder or place card, fold a piece of paper in half, trace the kangaroo shape in Pic. 1, and cut it out. Open and lay it carefully on a piece of Bristol board. Now draw around it. Cut it out and fold as indicated by dotted lines. Now color it to look like a kangaroo, using brown, tan, and black crayons or paints. Slip a small bottle, filled with tiny candy, in front of it for a pouch. To use as a place card, stand the kangaroo and bottle on a white card on which you've printed your guest's name in color. Heavy brown paper, such as grocer's bags, make good kangaroos, as they need only a little coloring to make them look quite real. A large one, made over this pattern, could be used as a gift holder. Replace the bottle with a big box.

Make-believe Money. Place a real coin under a piece of aluminum foil. Rub over it, gently but firmly, with an eraser so that the design on the coin is pressed onto the foil. Do both sides and paste these pieces to stiff paper cut to the size of the coin. Wonderful play money.

Pic. 1

Fold back →

← Fold forward

Fold forward

Cut to dot →

Fold up →

Fold back

49

Party Hats

Hats add much to the gaiety of any party, and making them is often the most fun of all. Look through your treasure box for materials you can use, such as shelf paper, tissue paper, crepe paper, and brown-paper bags. Little bells, legal seals, bits of ribbon or lace, and paper doilies are all useful. Only a few hats are shown on these pages, but once you get the hang of making them you will think of many different ones to do.

Pic. 1

15"

15"

Clown's Hat. This is attractive when made of colored paper. Cut a quarter circle, as shown in Pic. 1. Paste narrow, colored streamers to the point. Roll into a cone shape, overlapping enough to fit your head, as in Pic. 2. Fasten open sides together with an adhesive. For more clownlike effect draw a checkerboard design on the paper just before rolling it into shape.

Pic. 2

Overlap

Pic. 3

Pic. 4

Gather →

Overlap

Circle

Chef's Hat. Cut a strip of shelf paper, long enough to go around your head, with 2 inches to spare, and as high as you want your cap to be. Roll into a tube, overlapping 1 inch, as in Pic. 3. Paste in place. Measure the tube across and cut a tissue circle which measures three times as much across, as in Pic. 4. Gather the outer edge of this circle and glue to the inside of the tube, as in Pic. 5. Add a legal seal and colored-paper decoration.

Gather and glue here

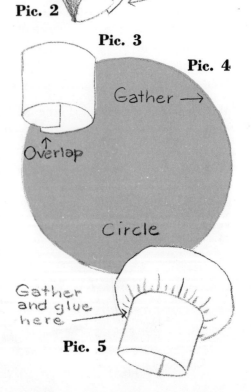

Pic. 5

50

An engineer's cap can be made from the directions for the chef's hat by cutting the band narrower and adding a visor instead of a decoration. For other kinds of hats, circle flowers, like the ones on pages 52 and 53, can be pasted to a strip of crepe paper and made into a crown. Any old felt hat can be cut into a nice shape and covered completely with these flowers. Use one of the new adhesives in making all these hats.

Pic. 1

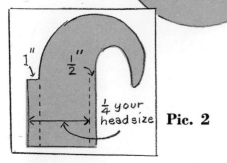

Pic. 2

Pic. 3

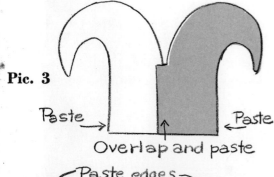

Paste → ← Paste

Overlap and paste

Paste edges

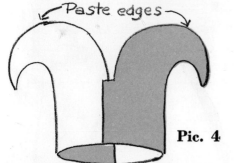

Pic. 4

Beret. Cut two tissue circles the size you want your beret to be when finished. Glue a 1-inch-wide strip of heavy paper into a ring that will fit around your head. Lay this ring in the center of one of the circles and draw around it. Now draw another ring 1 inch smaller; cut out and clip as shown in Pic. 1. Paste this clipped area to the inside of the headband. Use an adhesive to hold the two circles together at the edges.

Jester's Cap. This is most attractive when made of two different-colored papers. Draw a shape on a double piece of tissue, or other paper, as shown in Pic. 2. Trace this onto a double thickness of a different-color paper and cut them all out. You should have four pieces. Make front and back by pasting two different-colored pieces together, as in Pic. 3. Put front and back together with adhesive, as in Pic. 4. Add bits of tinsel or tiny bells to points. Sometimes these points need to be stuffed lightly with tissue to keep their shape.

Paper Flowers

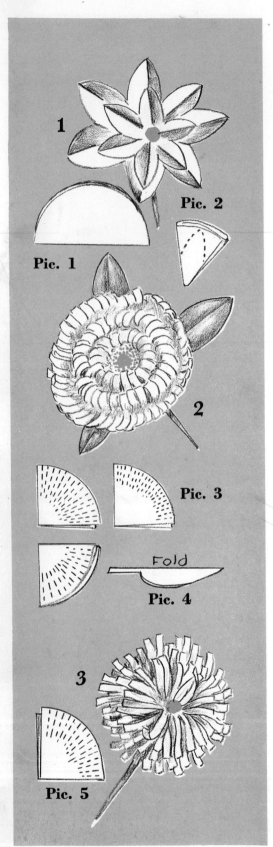

1

Pic. 1

Pic. 2

2

Pic. 3

Pic. 4

Fold

3

Pic. 5

These lovely flowers can be used in many attractive ways, such as table or house decorations, vase and basket fillers, party hats, picture frames, pictures, and greeting cards. All of the flowers on these pages are made from circles of different sizes. Many more than those shown can be made. Try folding, cutting, and shaping the basic circle in different sizes and ways, combining three or four in the same flower. Toothpicks, painted green, or wire make fine stems. Start with the patterns and directions on these pages and then you can go on to make flowers of your own design.

1. Cut two circles, one 2¾ inches across, the other 2 inches. Fold in half, as in Pic. 1. Fold again into three, so it looks like Pic. 2. Cut as indicated by dotted lines. Open, crease petals, and run a toothpick through the centers.

2. Use three circles which measure 2¾ inches across. Fold and cut, as indicated by dotted lines in Pic. 3. Curl edges toward center, making the inside one tighter than the outside ones. Run a toothpick through the centers and add two leaves, cut as in Pic. 4.

3. Use two or three circles of the same size. Fold in half twice and cut as shown in Pic. 5. Open circles and run a toothpick through the centers, holding them in place with a touch of cement. Bunch the circles together for a fluffy effect.

4. Start with three circles, one cut 2¾ inches across, another 2 inches, and the third ¾ inches. Fold and cut small one, as in Pic. 6; the larger ones, as indicated by dotted lines in Pic. 7. Open circles and curl petals gently toward centers, and press fringe on small one toward center. Run a toothpick through the center of each to look like the picture.

5. Fold a circle in half, then again, as in Pic. 8. Cut as indicated by dotted lines as in Pic. 9. Open and run a green toothpick through the center. This makes a lovely star-shaped flower.

6. Fold a circle, as in Pic. 1., on facing page. Fold again into thirds, and cut as indicated by dotted lines in Pic. 2. Open and crease petals on folds. Insert a toothpick, to which you have added a tiny colored wax ball or bead, through the center. This flower is lovely when made of white paper.

7. Use a circle which you have folded and cut, as in Pic. 10., make one cut to the center. Twist fine hairpins or wires around a toothpick, and add tiny beads to the ends, as in Pic. 11. Starting with the cut, roll the circle into a conelike shape and insert wired toothpick.

8. Make a cut to the center of a circle, as in Pic. 12. Attach wires to toothpick and roll paper circle around it, as for flower 7. Hold in place by a touch of cement.

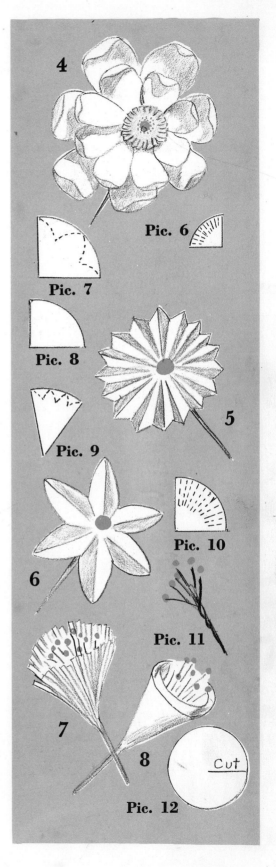

4

Pic. 6

Pic. 7

Pic. 8

Pic. 9

5

6

Pic. 10

Pic. 11

7

8

Pic. 12

Cut

Gifts and Toys

Maracas. Latin-American musical instruments made from gourds are called maracas. The dried seeds inside make a pleasant sound when the gourd is shaken in time to music. Use French-dressing bottles, which are shaped something like gourds, for make-believe maracas. Paint them in gay designs with bright-colored enamels, using small brushes. Add pebbles and beans for seeds.

Arm

Shoe

Pic. 1

Dancing Spool Doll. To make this doll you will need eight spools (six should be 1 inch high, one 2½ inches, the other 1½ inches); ten medium-large gold beads; a 60-inch length of elastic thread; a small curtain ring; some cotton, paint, and paper. Paint the six small spools olive green, the two others white, using show-card colors. Paint a face on the 1½-inch-size spool, and five red buttons on the other. Cut paper feet and arms, as in Pic. 1. Paint shoes red, sleeves green. To put the doll together, use a double strand of elastic thread about 30 inches long. Run through the curtain ring, then both ends through the head, two beads, and the body spool. To string the legs, separate the thread into two. Use four beads, three spools, and one shoe for each leg. Now, pull thread tight enough to hold spools together. Tie firm knots and cut off leftover threads. Add cotton for hair, and paste arms into place. Cover thread ends with Scotch tape attached to shoe soles.

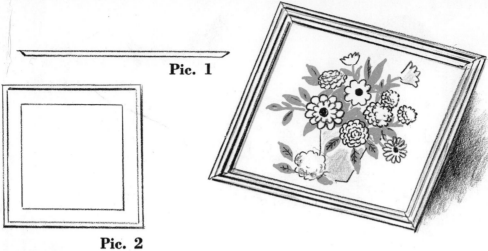

Pic. 1

Pic. 2

Drinking-straw Frame. Cut a cardboard frame about 8½ inches square and ¾ to 1 inch wide. Cut the corners from four white-paper drinking straws, as in Pic. 1. This is called mitering. Glue these straws to the outside edge of the frame, making corners meet, as in Pic. 2. Add rows of straws in this same way, measuring carefully before you cut ends, until the frame is covered. Add a hanger.

Tumbling Timmy. Cut six inches from a paper tube large enough to admit a golf ball. Cover the tube in white paper. Paint on a face and paste on pieces of rough cloth, such as velveteen or flannel, for a costume, as in Pic. 3. Cut two circles of the same cloth larger than the tube ends. Gather one and glue into place on the bottom end. Put an old golf ball into the tube. Gather and glue on the other circle to look like a hat. Cut cloth arms and legs and attach them as in the picture. This doll will tumble over and over on a rough incline.

Pic. 3

Tambourine. Punch three holes in each of two frozen-fruit-pie plates. Tie together with bright ribbon and add a bell through each knot so it looks like the picture on the right. This is fun to use along with the maracas on the facing page.

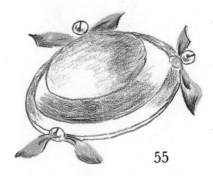

55

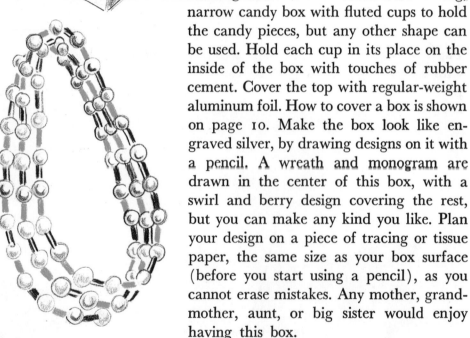

Earring Box. This is made from a long, narrow candy box with fluted cups to hold the candy pieces, but any other shape can be used. Hold each cup in its place on the inside of the box with touches of rubber cement. Cover the top with regular-weight aluminum foil. How to cover a box is shown on page 10. Make the box look like engraved silver, by drawing designs on it with a pencil. A wreath and monogram are drawn in the center of this box, with a swirl and berry design covering the rest, but you can make any kind you like. Plan your design on a piece of tracing or tissue paper, the same size as your box surface (before you start using a pencil), as you cannot erase mistakes. Any mother, grandmother, aunt, or big sister would enjoy having this box.

Necklace. Cut two cellophane drinking straws (one red, one green) into ¾-inch lengths and string into a necklace, using a large pearl bead between each straw section. You can make this a one-, two-, or three-strand necklace. Of course, the longer you want it the more straw sections and pearls you will need. This makes another good gift for Mother.

56

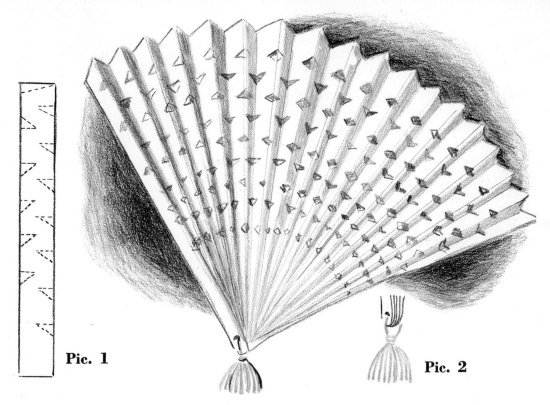

Pic. 1

Pic. 2

Paper Fan. Make fans like this one from almost any kind of paper with body enough to hold its shape. Try them in beautifully colored papers or in pure white, and don't forget that they can be made in any size. This one is made from a piece of coated, white shelf paper cut 20 by 10 inches. Fold into ½-inch accordion pleats and cut, as shown by dotted lines in Pic. 1. Open into a fan and hold together at the bottom by a tassel-like tie, made by running yarn through the fan and tying, as in Pic. 2. For an easier-to-make fan, fold the paper into larger-size pleats, or cut only on one side instead of both.

Piggy Bank. Start with a bread-crumb box or cheese box that has a top opening something like Pic. 3. Cover the bottom and sides of the box with white shelf paper. Add a white pipe-cleaner tail, paper ears, and legs cut from scraps of paste board or Styrofoam. Paint black spots on the body, and add eyes and a smiling mouth on the top. Twist the lid open to insert a coin. After the coins are inside, close the box and see how happy the pig looks.

Pic. 3

57

Pic. 1

Letter Holder. Cut the top from a small, firm detergent or cereal box to look like Pic. 1. Paint it inside and out with black enamel and let it dry. After it is thoroughly dry, decorate it with flowers, painted on with show-card colors and a fine brush, or use flowers cut from seed catalogues or magazines. Plan your designs carefully on pieces of tracing paper the size of the box surfaces. Trace these lightly onto the box before you start to paint. You may have to paint over the flower surfaces more than once to make them stand out.

Stamp or Pen Box. Dry mustard and several other spices come in small tins like the one shown. Use a small size which you have painted a dull black. Decorate this box any way you like, using show-card colors. The one on this page is decorated with a wreath and three initials, on both the back and front; a star form, made by crossed lines, on each side and in the corners of the top as well as on the lid. Band-Aid boxes can be decorated the same way.

String Dispenser. Cover a yogurt or cottage-cheese carton with pieces of any attractive paper you happen to have. Cut circles to fit both top and bottom. If you have an old map, it will make your dispenser most attractive. After the paper is pasted in position, apply two coats of color-less shellac, allowing to dry thoroughly between coats. Make a hole in the bottom, large enough for a string to slide through easily, and put a ball of string inside. Make a hole in the side, to hook over a nail, if you want to hang up the holder.

58

Pencil Holder. Cut a strip of corrugated paper 1¾ inches wide. The length you use will depend upon how large you want the holder to be. Roll the paper into a wheel, so it looks like the picture, and hold it in place with Scotch tape. Cover the sides with a piece of paper in a color which will look well with the rest of the things on the desk where it will be used. Paint on a name or initials.

Blotter-corner Covers. Cut a triangle from a heavy Manila envelope to measure 4¾ inches from the corner. Use a piece of colored paper, measuring 9½ by 7¾ inches. Fold a corner to fit into the open end of the triangle, as in Pic. 2. Now fold, as shown in Pic. 3 and 4. Fold remaining points into the open end of the triangle, as in Pic. 5. Make four of these to use on a desk as blotter corners. To cover in cloth, paste on triangles cut the same size as Manila corners. This is a very easy way to make a blotter-corner cover.

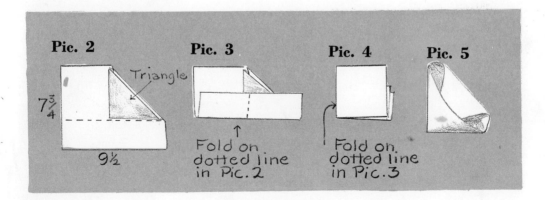

Pic. 2   Pic. 3   Pic. 4   Pic. 5

7¾   9½   Triangle   Fold on dotted line in Pic. 2   Fold on dotted line in Pic. 3

Pic. 1

Doll Chair. Start with a 3-inch section from a paper-towel tube cut as shown by dotted lines in Pic. 1. Cover it with cloth or paper, or paint it the color you want. Hold this over a piece of heavy white paper and draw around it to get a circle. Cut out and cover it the same as the rest of the chair and glue lightly into place for a seat. Glue on pieces of toothpicks for legs.

Make-believe Jewelry

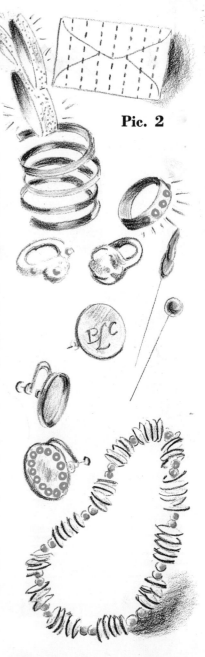

Pic. 2

BRACELETS. Cut the top and bottom from a small round can. Press the sides slightly to form an oval shape. Use it as it is, or cover with foil and scratch on initials. Use a twist, cut from the outside edge of a frozen-pie plate for a spiral bracelet. Cut a sealed envelope into sections, as indicated by dotted lines in Pic. 2. Sprinkle both sides with glitter and open each section into a paper bracelet.

RINGS. Fold gold foil into a band. Paste into a ring and glue on colored-foil stones. Twist foil into a dome-shaped ring. Hold together with a touch of glue. Press warm candle wax into a ring and glue on colored beads for stones.

PINS. Twist gold or silver foil over the head of a long pin, or run a long pin through a piece of warm wax; form the wax into a ball and allow it to harden. Then color the wax with green crayon for a jade effect. Cover an old circle pin with foil glued to a paper circle slightly larger than the pin. Scratch on initials.

EARRINGS. Twist pieces of colored foil into flat, stonelike pieces and glue to a pair of old earrings. Fasten beads or colored-wax pieces to earring backs.

NECKLACE. String old pearls and melon seeds into a necklace.

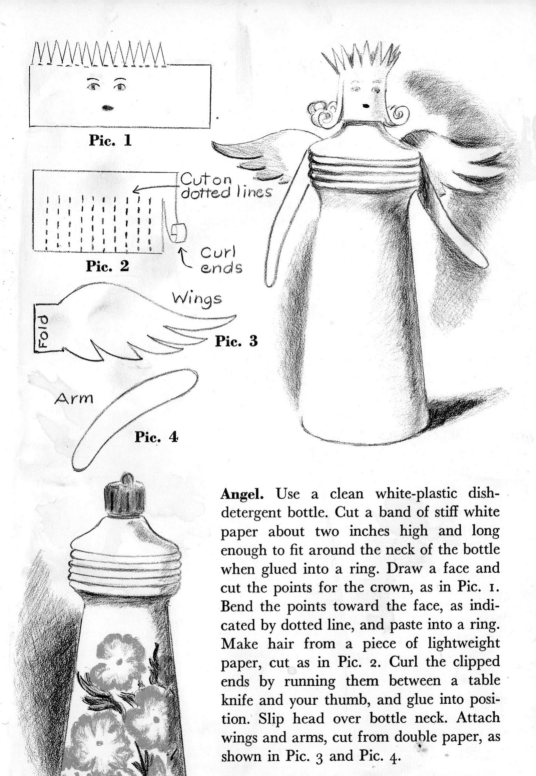

Pic. 1

Cut on dotted lines

Curl ends

Pic. 2

Wings

Fold

Pic. 3

Arm

Pic. 4

Angel. Use a clean white-plastic dish-detergent bottle. Cut a band of stiff white paper about two inches high and long enough to fit around the neck of the bottle when glued into a ring. Draw a face and cut the points for the crown, as in Pic. 1. Bend the points toward the face, as indicated by dotted line, and paste into a ring. Make hair from a piece of lightweight paper, cut as in Pic. 2. Curl the clipped ends by running them between a table knife and your thumb, and glue into position. Slip head over bottle neck. Attach wings and arms, cut from double paper, as shown in Pic. 3 and Pic. 4.

Watering Bottle. Paste colored flowers, cut from a seed catalogue, onto a clean dish-detergent bottle. Cover with a coat of clear shellac and use for watering small plants.

61